EPIDEMICS & PANDEMICS

THE SCIENCE OF THE HUMAN BODY

BODY SYSTEMS

CELLS, TISSUES & ORGANS

DISEASES

EPIDEMICS & PANDEMICS

GENES & GENETICS

IMMUNOLOGY

MASON CREST
450 Parkway Drive, Suite D, Broomall, Pennsylvania 19008
(866) MCP-BOOK (toll-free)

James Shoals

First printing
9 8 7 6 5 4 3 2 1

ISBN (hardback) 978-1-4222-4197-4
ISBN (series) 978-1-4222-4191-2
ISBN (ebook) 978-1-4222-7616-7

Cataloging-in-Publication Data on file with the Library of Congress

Developed and Produced by National Highlights Inc.
Interior and cover design: Torque Advertising + Design
Production: Michelle Luke

THE SCIENCE OF THE HUMAN BODY

EPIDEMICS & PANDEMICS

JAMES SHOALS

MASON CREST

KEY ICONS TO LOOK FOR:

 Words to Understand: These words with their easy-to-understand definitions will increase the reader's understanding of the text while building vocabulary skills.

 Sidebars: This boxed material within the main text allows readers to build knowledge, gain insights, explore possibilities, and broaden their perspectives by weaving together additional information to provide realistic and holistic perspectives.

 Educational videos: Readers can view videos by scanning our QR codes, providing them with additional educational content to supplement the text. Examples include news coverage, moments in history, speeches, iconic sports moments, and much more!

 Text-Dependent Questions: These questions send the reader back to the text for more careful attention to the evidence presented there.

Research Projects: Readers are pointed toward areas of further inquiry connected to each chapter. Suggestions are provided for projects that encourage deeper research and analysis.

QR CODES AND LINKS TO THIRD-PARTY CONTENT

You may gain access to certain third-party content ("Third-Party Sites") by scanning and using the QR Codes that appear in this publication (the "QR Codes"). We do not operate or control in any respect any information, products, or services on such Third-Party Sites linked to by us via the QR Codes included in this publication, and we assume no responsibility for any materials you may access using the QR Codes. Your use of the QR Codes may be subject to terms, limitations, or restrictions set forth in the applicable terms of use or otherwise established by the owners of the Third-Party Sites. Our linking to such Third-Party Sites via the QR Codes does not imply an endorsement or sponsorship of such Third-Party Sites or the information, products, or services offered on or through the Third-Party Sites, nor does it imply an endorsement or sponsorship of this publication by the owners of such Third-Party Sites.

CONTENTS

EPIDEMICS & PANDEMICS

Epidemics and pandemics are one of the biggest threats to the world and are responsible for killing millions of people. Epidemics are outbreaks of diseases that occur within enclosed geographical boundaries. On the other hand, pandemics occur on a larger scale and have the capacity to wipe out entire towns, villages, and human populations. Even after successful elimination, both epidemics and pandemics can reemerge and cause havoc.

Epidemic

According to the World Health Organization (WHO), an epidemic is the outbreak of a disease that spreads quickly and affects many people. A disease

WORDS TO UNDERSTAND

chronic: persistent.

acquired: here, refers to a trait the body develops after birth.

inherent: here, refers to traits that a body already had at birth.

can become an epidemic when people of an area do not have either an acquired or an inherent immunity to the disease. True epidemics are caused by infectious agents. However outbreaks of chronic diseases, such as cardiovascular diseases, are frequently also referred to as "epidemics."

Causes

Disease-causing microorganisms can spread in several ways, such as from one person to another, from animals to humans, and from inanimate objects like contaminated water. If a disease is introduced in a population by more than one means, it can spread rapidly, giving rise to an epidemic. Poor hygiene and sanitation as well as lack of proper healthcare facilities help in spreading the disease.

Pandemic

A pandemic is an infectious disease that affects large populations when an epidemic spreads across its geographical boundaries and begins to affect nearby regions. The word *pandemic* is derived from the Greek word *pandemos*, which means "pertaining to all people." All pandemics are epidemics but not all epidemics can be called pandemics because they are confined to a particular area.

What Makes a Disease Pandemic?

A medical condition or disease cannot be called a pandemic just because it affects a large number of people around the world. The disease has to be infectious. For example, obesity and heart disease are very common around the globe and are sometimes referred to as "epidemics" by the media. But they are not infectious and so they don't qualify as pandemics. According to the WHO, the outbreak of a disease can be called a pandemic when:

- **the disease has not affected the population before.**
- **the disease-causing microorganisms or agents spread easily.**
- **the disease causes severe illness and is life-threatening.**

Pandemic Stages

According to the Centers for Disease Control and Prevention (CDC), pandemic diseases have three stages: the interpandemic period, the pandemic alert period, and the pandemic period. In the interpandemic period, the disease is detected in new populations. Pandemic alert indicates that the disease has begun to spread. When the disease has been transmitted to the general population, it is called the pandemic period.

 SIDEBAR: DID YOU KNOW?

- **Some epidemics are contagious, some are not. But illnesses must be infectious to qualify as pandemics.**
- **The word *pandemic* is derived from the Greek word *pandemos*, meaning "pertaining to all people."**

HIV AND AIDS

Human Immunodeficiency Virus (HIV) is a virus that leads to a serious medical condition called Acquired Immunodeficiency Syndrome (AIDS). The virus is capable of **mutating** very quickly, so it becomes very difficult for the body to recognize it. This is why doctors are still not able to develop a vaccine to prevent it. It is one of the reasons that HIV and AIDS have become pandemic. Millions of people have succumbed to the disease while million of others are living with it.

How Does HIV Affect the Body?

When a person becomes infected with HIV, the virus attacks the immune system and destroys blood cells in the body called **lymphocytes**, or CD4 cells, also known as T cells. These cells are required by the body to fight off infections and diseases. When the number of T cells are reduced to a very low level, the immune system becomes extremely weak. This makes the affected person vulnerable to minor infections and diseases that

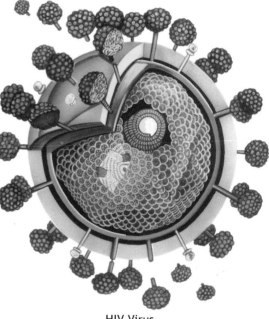

HIV Virus

 WORDS TO UNDERSTAND

lymphocytes: white blood cells that attack foreign bodies.
mutating: changing or evolving.
sterilize: to make something free from germs.

he would haven been able to fight off otherwise. AIDS is the advanced stage of the HIV infection and can take 10 to 15 years to develop. AIDS affects organ systems of the body, making its victims weaker with time.

Stages of HIV Infection

There are three stages of HIV infection.

Acute HIV: This stage lasts for one or two weeks after contracting the infection. People experience flu-like symptoms as the infection spreads rapidly throughout the body.

Asymptomatic HIV: This stage can last for years. The person does not have any symptoms and may not know he or she is infected.

Symptomatic HIV or AIDS: This stage lasts for one to three years. This is the stage in which the patient can become very ill with multiple diseases.

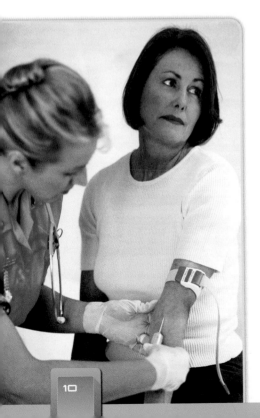

Means of Transmission

HIV can be transmitted from one person to another. Having multiple sexual partners or unprotected sex are typical ways of HIV transmission. Physical relations with someone suffering from HIV or other sexually transmitted diseases (STDs) increase the chances of contracting the virus. Sharing contaminated needles or syringes used by an HIV-infected person is another common means of transmission. HIV can also be transmitted during blood transfusions if the equipment is not **sterilized**, or by a woman to her baby during pregnancy, childbirth, or breastfeeding.

Prevention and Cure

There is no cure for HIV/AIDS, so prevention is very important. Multiple sexual partners or unprotected sex must be avoided. Don't use intravenous drugs. If HIV has been contracted, the patient should undergo a treatment called antiretroviral therapy to keep the virus under control. The patient should regularly take antiviral drugs and other drugs that boost the immune system.

Find out more about the virus that causes HIV.

MUTATIONS

10 BILLION NEW VIRONS / DAY

SIDEBAR: DID YOU KNOW?

- **HIV is a lentivirus, which means takes a long time to bring any adverse effects on the body.**

- **HIV can only transmit through direct contact because the virus cannot survive outside the body.**

HISTORY OF HIV/AIDS

1980: It is believed that HIV originated in Africa and gradually spread to other parts of the world. The disease broke out in Uganda in the early 1980s and became an epidemic, infecting and killing millions of people. High population, poor **sanitation**, illiteracy, and a lack of medical facilities helped HIV to become an epidemic in Africa. The continent continues to be very heavily affected with HIV and AIDS compared to the rest of the world.

1980

1981

1981: Several cases of pneumonia caused by a new type of bacteria and a rare type of skin cancer known as Kaposi's sarcoma came to light in the United States. The illness was observed in people with a weak immune system. It was most common in **homosexual** men and by the end of the year, 270 cases of severe immune system deficiency were reported, out of which 121 patients died. The medical condition was termed as gay-related immune deficiency (GRID).

 WORDS TO UNDERSTAND

homosexual: a person attracted to the person of the same sex.
retrovirus: a type of virus that reproduces by inserting its genetic material into a host cell.
sanitation: conditions related to people's health and hygiene, which involves the provision of clean water supply as well as waste management.

1983: Françoise Barré-Sinoussi discovered the **retrovirus** responsible for causing AIDS. Later, two research groups led by Robert Gallo and Luc Montagnier also discovered the cause of the disease. Gallo called the virus HTLV-III (human T-lymphotropic virus), whereas Montagnier called it LAV (lymphadenopathy-associated virus). That same year, reports about the spread of AIDS were coming from France, Australia, Britain, and Africa. Altogether, 33 countries reported cases of the illness. The CDC made it clear that the disease could be transferred through blood transfusion and from an expecting mother to her newborn during childbirth. The CDC also encouraged people to avoid sharing needles for drug use.

| 1982 | 1983 | 1987 | 1990 |

1982: It was found that the disease was not restricted to the gay community. Heterosexuals and even children were contracting the HIV virus. Therefore, the term GRID was misleading and the CDC redefined the illness and coined the term Acquired Immunodeficiency Syndrome (AIDS). In several European countries, reports of the occurrence of HIV/AIDS were on the rise.

1987: By now, 71,616 people were diagnosed with AIDS and 41,262 had died. The Food and Drug Administration (FDA) of the US approved the first antiretroviral drug—zidovudine (AZT).

1990: According to the WHO, there were almost nine million people living with HIV around the world in the early 1990s. This number increased up to 30 million by 1997. According to the CDC, AIDS became the leading cause of death of people aged 25 to 44 years in the United States.

2000: In Africa, about 22.2 million people have contracted HIV, which accounts for two-thirds of the total number of people affected by HIV in the world at this point. The number has increased since then.

2000   2015   * according to most recent reporting

2015: A UN report announced that 15.8 million people were undergoing treatment with antiretroviral drugs. This demonstrated a huge increase of the number of HIV-positive people who were able to access treatment—it's more than twice the number getting treated just five years earlier.

SIDEBAR: DID YOU KNOW?

- In 2017, more than 20 million people globally were undergoing treatment for HIV/AIDS.
- December 1 is recognized as the World AIDS Day by the WHO.

NUTRITION AND HIV/AIDS

HIV and nutrition are interlinked—one affects the other in a positive or negative way. HIV infection leads to **malnutrition**, and malnutrition weakens the immune system and aggravates the effects of HIV. Malnutrition is recognized as one of the key factors that contributes to the rapid progression of AIDS. Nutrition plays an important role in supporting AIDS-affected people.

Malnutrition and HIV

Malnutrition can both cause and result from the progression of HIV. A malnourished person who acquires HIV is likely to progress faster to AIDS than his healthy counterpart. Malnutrition severely affects the ability of the immune system to offer

 WORDS TO UNDERSTAND

anorexia: loss of appetite.

chronic: a serious illness that lasts for a long time or reoccurs frequently.

malnutrition: the state of being undernourished; having insufficient vitamins, protein, and so on.

metabolism: a chemical process in the body that helps cells in producing energy and other substances necessary for life.

resistance to various infections. The body, already weak and worn out, is in no condition to fight the HIV infection. A well-nourished person has a stronger immune system to help him cope with HIV.

How does HIV Cause Malnutrition

A person infected with HIV is highly susceptible to malnutrition due to several reasons.

• **Changes in metabolism and poor absorption of nutrients:** HIV results in a weaker digestive system and poor absorption of nutrients (proteins, carbohydrates, fats, vitamins, minerals, and water).

• **Chronic infections and illnesses:** A number of infections and illnesses like fever, diarrhea, tuberculosis, flu, and stomach infections accompany HIV. They can further deplete the nutrients and lead to malnutrition.

• **Anorexia:** Due to infections and illnesses, anorexia, or loss of appetite is common in HIV patients. Social and emotional pressure may also reduce the appetite and accelerate malnutrition.

Nutritional Needs of HIV Patients

People suffering from AIDS require ample amounts of nutrients like proteins, carbohydrates, fats, minerals, and vitamins. Protein-energy

malnutrition—a deficiency of fats and proteins—causes weight loss and wasting. As a result, HIV patients need more nutrition. They need to increase their energy intake by 10 to 15 percent and protein intake by 50 to 100 percent as compared to those without HIV.

Nutritional Practices for HIV Patients

A nutritious diet helps maintain the proper functioning of the immune system. A balanced diet certainly cannot cure AIDS, but it will increase life expectancy and help patients lead a better life. Certain habits like eating small, frequent meals and including a variety of foods in the diet can be of great help.

Small and Frequent Meals

Eating small and frequent meals can help HIV patients in better absorption of nutrients. Instead of three big meals, they should eat several smaller meals. Healthy snacking throughout the day can help to increase the intake of food. HIV patients require softer and moister foods that can be digested easily.

Variety in Foods

HIV patients should eat a balanced diet consisting of both plant and animal foods. Consuming a variety of foods, such as legumes, nuts, fruits, and vegetables, from all the food groups, will help them against high-risk infections and diseases. It will also help in stabilizing body weight.

SIDEBAR: DID YOU KNOW?

- Eating a variety of foods can ensure that an individual gets all the essential nutrients.
- In families affected by AIDS, food consumption can drop by 40 percent due to decreased earnings.

INFLUENZA

Influenza is a viral infection of the respiratory tract. The virus enters the body through the nose or mouth and attacks the throat, bronchi, and lungs. Unlike other viral infections of the respiratory tract such as the common cold, influenza can cause severe illness. It is also highly **contagious** and spreads rather quickly. Most people down with influenza can recover completely in one or two weeks. However, the disease can be **fatal** in the case of elderly people, infants, or those with chronic illness. The disease is commonly known as the "flu." Birds and animals also suffer from influenza.

Types of Influenza Viruses

There are three types of influenza viruses: A, B, and C. Type A and B cause epidemics of respiratory infection and occur in almost every winter. They infect a large number of people and can even cause death. Type C virus, on the other hand, is responsible for causing mild respiratory illness and it might or might not show any symptoms.

Influenza Virus

 WORDS TO UNDERSTAND

contagious: communicable or easily transmitted from one person to the other.

fatal: leading to or causing death.

nausea: to feel sick and an inclination to vomit.

How Does it Spread?

Like other viruses, the influenza virus enters the body through mouth, nose, or breaks in the skin. Then the virus attacks cells and replicates inside them. When the replication is complete, the virus bursts open the host cells, and eventually kills them. After some time, the infected person begins to show the symptoms.

Types of Influenza

- **Seasonal influenza:** occurs annually, in late winter and fall.
- **Avian influenza:** occurs in birds and does not spread from birds to humans.
- **Pandemic influenza:** occurs at any time of the year and is highly contagious.

Means of Transmission

Influenza can be transmitted by coming into direct contact with people suffering from the disease. One can become infected by inhaling respiratory droplets from the cough or sneeze of infected people, or by sharing their towels or utensils. Even touching any contaminated surfaces such as doorknobs or sharing bedrooms or bathrooms increases the chances of the transmission of flu.

Symptoms of Influenza

The influenza virus has a very short incubation span (about one to two days) and the symptoms appear very soon. Fever, chills, body ache, headache, cough, sneeze, sore throat, and runny nose are a few of the early signs. However, the infected person may also suffer from dizziness, weakness, **nausea**, loss of appetite, vomiting, and diarrhea.

Prevention and Cure

To avoid catching the flu, people should get themselves vaccinated. It is the most effective preventive measure. An updated influenza vaccine is available as a shot or nasal mist every year. Good personal hygiene is important. Hands should be washed often with soap and water, especially after using restrooms, coughing or sneezing, and before and after eating. Avoid sharing food and drinks or utensils with those suffering from flu. People should avoid using tissues that have already been used and always cover their mouth and nose while coughing or sneezing. Drinking lots of water and fruit juice to prevent dehydration and getting plenty of rest help in reducing the effects of influenza.

SIDEBAR: DID YOU KNOW?

- **The flu shot and nasal mist contains killed flu viruses that will not cause the flu, but prepare the body to fight off infection by the live flu virus.**

- **Millions of Americans suffer from influenza every year.**

HISTORY OF INFLUENZA

Studies on animal diseases resulted in the chance discovery of influenza. It is believed that humans became infected with influenza when the domestication of animals began. A virus closely related to the disease in humans can be found in pigs, ducks, chickens, and turkeys. The earliest human influenza is supposed to have occurred about 6,000 years ago. However, the human influenza virus was not isolated until 1933.

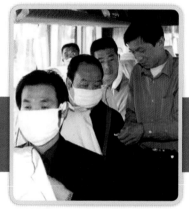

1485

Flu in Britain – 1485

In 1485, a wave of flu-like disease swept across Britain, which was referred to as "sweating sickness." The Lord Mayor of London, his **successor**, and six council members all died of the disease. The Royal Navy could not go on missions because the sailors had fallen sick after contracting the flu. Doctors around Britain advised patients to drink lime juice and tobacco juice in order to cure the illness.

 WORDS TO UNDERSTAND

gauze: a thin fabric.
Iberian: relating to Spain and Portugal.
peninsula: a piece of land almost entirely surrounded by water.
successor: someone who follows someone else in a job.

Flu in Asia – 1580

The first well-recorded flu pandemic occurred in Asia in 1580 and was so severe that it crossed physical boundaries and reached Europe, Africa, and America. The flu epidemic first arose in Asia Minor and Northern Africa. According to historical records from Italy, the disease spread from Malta to Sicily in July 1580, and then reached north through the Italian **peninsula** by August. Philip II ruled the **Iberian** Peninsula, Southern Italy, and several African ports during that time. He sent his troops to the Spanish Netherlands to fight the Dutch. His troops most likely spread influenza in the region. Over 90 percent of the populations of those areas were afflicted. The mortality rate was very high and many Spanish cities were wiped out.

1580

1729-82

Flu in the 18th Century – 1729-82

During the 18th century, three pandemics occurred between 1729-1730, 1732-1733, and 1781-1782. The 1729-1730 flu pandemic was one of the first recorded pandemics in human history. The pandemic was further spread as people traveled from one place to the other. However, it did not prove to be fatal and the mortality rate was very low. In 1732-1733, flu broke out in North America and reached New England, from Boston to Maine.

Russian Flu – 1729-82

The Russian flu probably originated in China in 1889, and spread quickly to Russia and throughout Europe. Then it advanced towards North America in December 1889 and reached Latin America and Asia in February 1890. The pandemic took the lives of about one million people.

The most destructive and widespread of the three pandemics was the pandemic of 1781-1782. It could be compared with the Russian flu of 1889 and the Spanish flu of 1918. The 1781-1782 flu originated during the spring in North Africa and North America in 1781. Then it spread to the eastern hemisphere and extensive outbreaks occurred in China and India during the fall. Then the pandemic spread further westwards in early 1782.

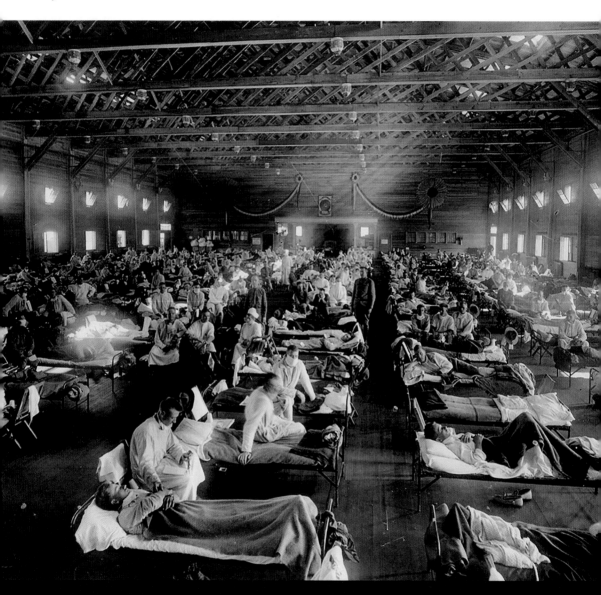

Historical photo of the 1918 Spanish influenza ward at Camp Funston, Kansas, showing the many patients ill with the flu.

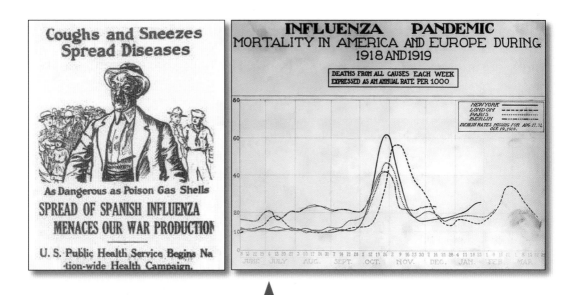

Coughs and Sneezes Spread Diseases

As Dangerous as Poison Gas Shells

SPREAD OF SPANISH INFLUENZA MENACES OUR WAR PRODUCTION

U. S. Public Health Service Begins Na·tion-wide Health Campaign.

INFLUENZA PANDEMIC
MORTALITY IN AMERICA AND EUROPE DURING 1918 AND 1919

DEATHS FROM ALL CAUSES EACH WEEK EXPRESSED AS AN ANNUAL RATE PER 1000

1918-19

Spanish Flu – 1918-19

The flu in Spain was a global catastrophe. It took the lives of 40 to 50 million people and was one of the worst pandemics in history. The disease, which was usually only life-threatening for children and old people, infected and killed young, healthy adults as well. The Spanish flu was caused by type A influenza virus. After research, many scientists believe that the virus came from birds and that it was similar to the Avian flu.

The origin of the Spanish flu virus is still unknown. However, it is speculated that the first wave of Spanish flu swept across the US in March 1918 in military camps. Not many people noticed the epidemic amid the world war. A cook in the U.S. Army reported sick at Fort Riley, Kansas, on March 4. By noon, over 100 soldiers had reported falling ill. After two weeks, about 522 men at the camp became ill. This was supposed to be the first recorded outbreak of influenza, which later came to be known as the Spanish flu. The disease was called the "Spanish flu" because Spanish newspapers were the first to talk about the outbreak. In addition, the flu also killed eight million people in Spain.

Impact of War on the Flu

In 1918, the first outbreak of the Spanish flu coincided with World War I. The soldiers in military camps were living under difficult and unhygienic conditions. Initially, the symptoms of the flu were confused with the common cold, but soon it was realized that the disease was far more dangerous. In the next two years, the Spanish flu affected large populations and almost one fifth of the entire world population was infected.

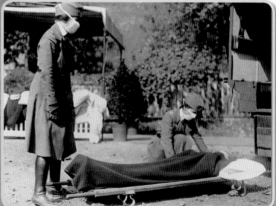

PREVENT DISEASE

CARELESS
SPITTING, COUGHING, SNEEZING,
SPREAD INFLUENZA
and TUBERCULOSIS

RENSSELAER COUNTY TUBERCULOSIS ASSOCIATION, TROY, N.Y.

Effects of the Pandemic

The massive pandemic forced public health departments to distribute **gauze** masks to people. Schools were closed and public gatherings were banned. Department stores could not sell their products and some shopkeepers closed down their stores. There was a lack of healthcare workers and medical supplies. In addition, there was a shortage of coffins, morticians, and gravediggers. Funerals were often restricted to as little as 15 minutes. In many places, mass graves were dug and the deceased were buried without coffins.

Find out what we can learn about current flu epidemics by studying past ones.

 SIDEBAR: DID YOU KNOW?

- Hippocrates, a great Greek physician, described a flu-like disease in 412 BC.
- The Spanish flu killed more people in a single year than the Black Death in the four years from 1347 to 1351.

RECENT FLU PANDEMICS

Influenza pandemics occur repeatedly and kill thousands of people around the globe. Apart from the seasonal flu epidemics, flu pandemics are less regular but can be deadly.

Asian Flu (1957–1958) H2N2

In February 1957, a flu epidemic broke out in the Far East. Soon the flu became a pandemic and reached the United States in the summer of 1957. The disease spread rapidly among schoolchildren, who passed on the infection to their families during the fall. There was a sudden rise in flu cases, which declined considerably by December 1957. However, a second wave of Asian flu rose in the early 1958 and killed about 70,000 people in the United States and about two million people around the world.

WORDS TO UNDERSTAND

considerably: a noticeable amount.
immunity: here, refers to the ability to resist an infection.

Hong Kong Flu (1968–1969)

The Hong Kong flu outbreak occurred in 1968 and spread gradually. The mortality rate peaked in December 1968 and January 1969. The virus known as H3N2 caused 700,000 deaths worldwide, including about 34,000 deaths in the US.

This flu pandemic caused fewer deaths than the previous flu pandemics for a variety of reasons.

• The influenza virus that caused the outbreak of the pandemic was a little similar to the virus that caused the Asian flu. Therefore, people had acquired some **immunity** against the Hong Kong flu virus.

• By December, there was a huge rise in the number of infections but since schoolchildren were on vacation, the disease did not spread on as large a scale as it might have otherwise.

• Drugs were available for treating secondary bacterial infections.

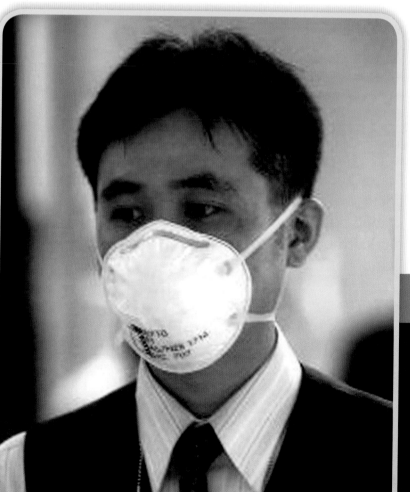

H1N1 or Swine Flu (2009-2010)

H1N1 flu is also known as swine flu since early laboratory tests showed that the flu virus was similar to the one that infects pigs (swine) in North America. However, further study made clear that the H1N1 virus is a different one. The first case of H1N1 was reported in Mexico in March 2009. In June 2009, swine flu was declared a pandemic by the WHO, when cases were reported in 74 countries. By the end of the year, according to the WHO, more than 200 regions in the world were affected by the flu and more than 18,000 people had died of it.

An earlier case of swine flu had been reported at Fort Dix, New Jersey, in 1976. One person died and four became ill but recovered. People called it the "killer flu" because many scientists and healthcare officials thought it to be similar to the Spanish flu of 1918-1919. However, H1N1 has not proven as deadly as the Spanish flu. Most people who contract swine flu recover.

SIDEBAR: DID YOU KNOW?

- You can't catch swine flu from eating pork.
- In 2009, the Egyptian government ordered the slaughter of all the pigs in the country to control the spread of H1N1— even though no cases of swine flu had been confirmed.

PLAGUE

Plague is an infectious zoonotic disease of animals and humans caused by the bacterium *Yersinia pestis*. The bacteria are found mostly in rodents, and in the fleas that feed on them. When the flea bites, it disgorges the bacteria into the bloodstream of the host. Other fleas then pick up the bacteria from the infected host and continue spreading the disease when biting others.

Types of Plague

There are three types of plague: bubonic, septicemic, and pneumonic plague. Bubonic plague is the infection that causes inflammation in the lymph nodes, which are vital parts of the immune system. Septicemic plague, on the other hand, is the infection of blood where bacteria multiply in the bloodstream. When the plague-causing bacteria infect lungs and cause pneumonia, it is called pneumonic plague. Pneumonic plague is highly contagious. However, it is not very common.

WORDS TO UNDERSTAND

inflammation: the reaction of a living tissue to an attack by a pathogenic organism, characterized by heat, swelling, and pain.

lymph nodes: part of the immune system that recognizes germs and fights them.

malaise: feeling weak, tired, or lethargic, especially during illness.

zoonotic: a type of disease than spreads from animals to humans.

Means of Transmission

A person can contract plague on being bitten or scratched by a plague-infected flea. Contact with infected animals such as rodents, cats, or dogs also helps the transmission of the disease. In fact, coming into direct contact with the blood or tissues of a diseased animal is also dangerous. Direct contact with those suffering from plague and breathing in infected droplets originating from coughs, sneezes, or the spit of infected people or animals also pose considerable danger. In addition, unhygienic living conditions increase the chances of disease transmission.

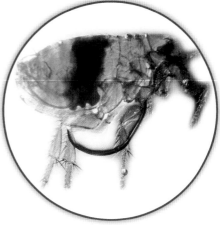

Symptoms of Plague

Flu-like symptoms appear within two to seven days after the infection. If bubonic plague is not treated in time, the bacteria spread and multiply into the bloodstream and can produce septicemic plague. Fever, chills, headache, muscle ache, vomiting, nausea, and malaise are some of the early signs and symptoms of plague. Lymph nodes also swell and painful lumps form, which are called bubo.

Prevention and Cure

Plague is a curable disease that can be treated with medication if diagnosed in time. However, if treatment does not start within 24 hours of the appearance of the first symptoms, the disease may prove to be fatal. Doctors usually prescribe antibiotics to treat the disease. According to medical research, about 50 percent of patients suffering from bubonic plague die if not treated.

People should follow some preventive measures to keep plague at bay. Maintaining good hygiene and sanitation in and around one's house and neighborhood is one of the main ways to prevent diseases. This will reduce the number of plague-causing agents, such as rodents and fleas. Insect repellents should be used and personal hygiene should be practiced.

Find out how the plague has affected the course of history.

SIDEBAR: DID YOU KNOW?

- *Yersinia pestis* lives in the stomach of the oriental rat flea, *Xenopsylla cheopis*.
- Alexandre Yersin, a physician and bacteriologist, discovered *Yersinia pestis* in 1894.

HISTORY OF PLAGUE

The first plague pandemic is believed to have originated in Ethiopia. It then spread to Egypt and other places through trade routes. The disease took the form of pestilence and reached the Byzantine Empire around 540-590 AD under the reign of Emperor Justinian. It was called the Plague of Justinian for that reason. Trade routes and military movements continued to spread the disease, which turned into a widespread pandemic, killing hundreds of thousands of people.

1334

Black Death - 1334

The Black Death was the most devastating pandemic in the human history. The epidemic broke out in China in 1334 and spread around the world. It spread through the movements of troops and trade merchants. The disease reached Europe from the cities of Genoa (northern Italy), Constantinople (Istanbul and Turkey), and the island of Sicily. It spread to these parts through trade routes linked to the Middle East where plague had been an epidemic since ancient times. The Europeans suffered the outbreak of bubonic plague from 1346 to 1350. It was called the Black Death because it blackened the victims' skin. Europe's population was reduced by at least 30 and perhaps as much as 60 percent.

WORDS TO UNDERSTAND

Byzantine Empire: the eastern half of the ancient Roman Empire.

contagion: describes the spread of a disease.

hamper: set back or damage.

Continued Outbreaks – 1361-1528

Plague continued to spread throughout the middle of the 15th century. Frequent outbreaks of plague hampered daily lives and damaged economies. Plague wrecked havoc on Europe and Russia, and continued to occur in other parts of the world. About 22 plague outbreaks occurred in Venice between 1361 and 1528. Another great outbreak of 1576-77 proved to be very deadly, killing 50,000 people.

1361-1528

1655

The Great Plague of London – 1655

The last major outbreak of plague affecting Europe occurred in London in 1665 and was known as the Great Plague. It first appeared in February and killed one-fifth of the population in the next seven months. By September, the death toll had risen up to 8,000 per week. Many Londoners fled the city, and those who had contracted the disease were forced to remain in their houses. In fact, their houses were painted with a red cross, with the words, "Lord, have mercy upon us." Hundreds of cats and dogs were killed as they were considered a source of contagion. Public meetings and social events were cancelled to prevent further spread of the disease.

Third Plague Pandemic – 1850s

The third major plague pandemic swept across China in the mid-19th century. It broke out in the Yunnan Province in 1855 and reached Hong Kong and Guangzhou rapidly, which were major trade centers. Soon the disease spread to port cities through the rodents on trade ships. This accelerated the spread of plague throughout the world. About ten million people around the world succumbed to the disease.

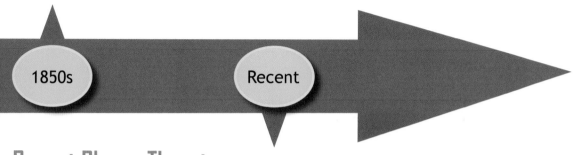

1850s

Recent

Recent Plague Threats

In recent times, there have been small outbreaks of plague around the world. The disease is found in many African, Asian, and South American countries. Globally between the years 2010 and 2015, there were 3,248 cases of plague reported, and 584 people died.

SIDEBAR: DID YOU KNOW?

- Half the population of Paris succumbed to the Black Death.
- The period of the Black Death was referred to as "the Great Mortality" by Europeans and "the Year of Annihilation" by people in the Muslim world.

MALARIA

Malaria is a life-threatening **parasitic** disease transmitted by female mosquitoes of the genus *Anopheles*. It is prevalent in tropical and subtropical regions as a significant amount of rainfall and hot temperatures provide the perfect setting for the mosquitoes to breed. When an infected mosquito bites, it transmits malaria parasites to its victim, who falls ill. Other mosquitoes then pick up the parasite from the infected person and continue spreading the disease as they bite other people.

Life Cycle of the Parasite

When a female mosquito ingests the malarial parasite *Plasmodium*, it takes about 10 to 12 days to develop fully. The duration of development also depends upon the type of parasite species, temperature and humidity levels. Higher temperatures promote early growth of the parasite. The mosquito can only become a **vector** of malaria if the parasite

 WORDS TO UNDERSTAND

endemic: regularly found.
parasitic: relating to or caused by parasites.
vector: an organism that carries diseases.

has developed fully. The parasite, in the form of gametocytes, divides rapidly inside a mosquito. They multiply in the salivary glands of the mosquito and develop into sporozoites. When the mosquito bites a person, these sporozoites travel through his bloodstream and the infection continues to spread.

What Causes Malaria?

Malaria is caused by any of four parasites: *Plasmodium vivax, Plasmodium ovale, Plasmodium malariae* and *Plasmodium falciparum*. It is transmitted to humans from the bite of the female Anopheles mosquito. After a person has been infected with the disease, he can spread malaria to other people through blood transfusion. Organ transplantation is another means through which infection can be transmitted. Using shared needles or syringes contaminated with infected blood can also pass the malarial infection. An expecting mother down with malaria can transmit the infection to her unborn child. This type of malaria is called congenital malaria.

Prevention and Cure

Malaria can be cured by taking antimalarial drugs such as chloroquine or quinine, which can be taken orally, by injection, or intravenously.
To prevent the spread of the disease, measures should be adopted to control mosquito-breeding. Stagnant water should be drained out, containers that might collect water should be removed, and water tanks should be covered with lids. People should use mosquito repellants to kill mosquitoes inside the house and insecticides in and around the house to destroy their breeding sites. They should wear protective clothing while sleeping and sleep under insecticide-treated mosquito nets. Traveling to areas where malaria is **endemic** should be avoided if possible.

Effects on Humans

Malaria symptoms usually appear from 10 to 12 days after the mosquito bite. However, severe malaria can cause anemia, jaundice, acute kidney failure, coma, or even death. Some of its early symptoms are as high fever and flu-like illness, excessive shivering, sweating, headache, and nausea. Infected people can also suffer from muscle ache, tiredness, and diarrhea.

 SIDEBAR: DID YOU KNOW?

- More than two thirds of malaria deaths occur in children under age five.
- The word *malaria* emerged from the Italian words *mala aria,* which mean "bad air."

HISTORY OF MALARIA

Malaria has been infecting people since ancient times. Both the malaria parasite and malaria-spreading mosquitoes have always been present. It was believed that the disease originated in Africa and spread to Southeast Asia, India, and South America through human migration. The ancient Greek physician, Hippocrates, described the nature of malaria fevers and associated it with swamps and marshlands in 400 BC.

Roman Fever

Malaria was one of the main causes of the decline of the Roman Empire. While the disease had always affected people there, malaria became an epidemic when the empire began to fall apart. Favorable conditions for mosquito-breeding such as **stagnant** water, marshes, swamps, drainage problems, and unsanitary surroundings promoted the spread the disease. Malaria became so **prevalent** that people began calling it the "Roman Fever."

First Recorded Treatment

People began to treat malaria as early as the 1600s. The Peruvian Indians were the first to treat the disease with the help of a tree bark known to have medicinal qualities. The wife of the Viceroy of Peru—Countess of

 WORDS TO UNDERSTAND

Jesuits: an order of Roman Catholic priests.
prevalent: common or widespread.
stagnant: unmoving.

Chinchón—was cured of her fever with this bark. The tree was named Cinchona in honor of the countess. The bark contained a substance called quinine. Soon, many people learned about it and the Jesuits introduced the treatment to Europe in the 1640s. Even today, quinine is the most recommended antimalaria medicine.

Malaria Discoveries

In 1880, Alphonse Laveran, a French army surgeon, discovered that malaria is caused because of parasites. He discovered parasites in the blood of malaria patients

Ronald Ross discovered the malaria parasite

and published his great finding in 1884. Laveran also said that the marsh fever parasite must undergo one stage of development in mosquitoes. His mosquito theory became the studying ground for Ronald Ross, a British army surgeon. Ross studied malaria patients and mosquitoes and soon discovered the malaria parasite inside mosquitoes. In 1897, he demonstrated that mosquitoes transmit the malaria parasite. Both Laveran and Ross were given the Nobel Prize for their great work.

Malaria Today

Malaria is endemic in more than 90 countries and every year more than 200 million cases of malaria are reported worldwide. Africa is the worst affected; the vast majority of all malaria cases are reported from the sub-Saharan regions. Poor healthcare services and unsanitary conditions are some of the reasons why malaria is still widespread. In 2016, 445,000 people died of the disease.

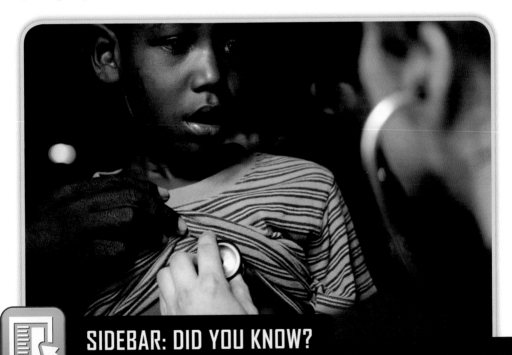

SIDEBAR: DID YOU KNOW?

- Urticaria pigmentosa, a skin disease, is caused by excessive working of mast cells in infants.
- Neutrophils reach the site of injury within an hour.

WEST NILE VIRUS

The West Nile Virus is a viral disease that can cause infection in the brain and the spinal cord. Before 1999, it was prevalent only in Africa, Asia, and Southern Europe. In 1999, it moved to the US and caused severe illness. This disease was first identified in a woman in the West Nile district of Uganda in 1937. It was named after the region of its origin.

Transmission

Like malaria, West Nile is a virus transmitted to humans from the bite of infected mosquitoes. The virus enters the blood stream of mosquitoes when they feed on infected birds. It enters their **salivary glands**. The virus enters the bloodstream of humans when the infected mosquitoes bite them. Many mosquito species act as carriers of this virus. *Culex pipiens*, or the common house mosquitoes, are the primary transmitters. The risk of getting West Nile increases in high temperatures and decreases as the weather becomes colder.

 WORDS TO UNDERSTAND

encephalitis: inflammation of the brain.
meningitis: inflammation of the lining of the brain and spinal cord.
salivary glands: glands that secrete a liquid, saliva, into the mouth.

Transmisson Cycle

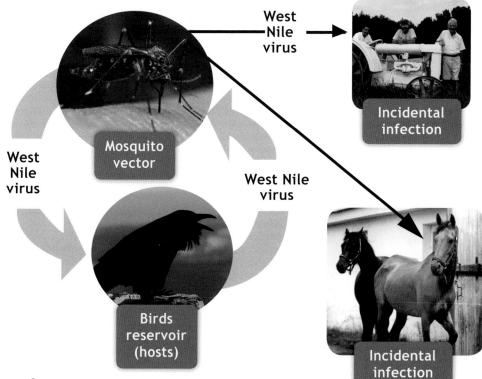

West Nile virus

Incidental infection

West Nile virus

Mosquito vector

West Nile virus

Birds reservoir (hosts)

Incidental infection

Symptoms

Most infected people show mild symptoms, such as flu-like fever, headache, muscle ache, tiredness, and joint pain. Some people may also develop a mild rash or swollen glands. In extreme cases, this infection causes serious illnesses such as meningitis or encephalitis. Small children, older people, and those with a weakened immune system due to AIDS, cancer, or organ transplants are at the highest risk. According to some calculations, approximately 1 in 150 persons infected with the West Nile virus develops a more severe form of the disease.

Treatment

At present, there is no treatment that can kill the West Nile Virus. There is no vaccine for this disease and antibiotics do not help to treat it, either. In mild cases, treatment mainly includes rest and drinking plenty of fluids. In severe cases, treatment involves hospitalization, intravenous fluids, and respiratory support.

Precautions

In the absence of a vaccine, the only way to reduce infection in people is by increasing awareness and educating them about the measures they can take to lessen exposure to the virus. People should ensure protection against mosquito bites by using mosquito nets, insect repellents, wearing light-colored clothing (long-sleeved shirts and trousers) and avoiding outdoor activities during the peak season. Water should not be allowed to accumulate because stagnant water becomes the breeding ground for mosquitoes.

The Biggest Outbreak in History

The West Nile Virus first appeared in 1999 in New York. From there, it spread to 46 more states and Washington, D.C. The greatest number of cases were reported from five states—Texas, Mississippi, Louisiana, Oklahoma, and Illinois— with the highest incidence of the disease in Texas. As of January 2018, slightly more than 2,000 cases had been reported in the United States.

 SIDEBAR: DID YOU KNOW?

- The virus can cause severe disease and even death in horses. Vaccines are available for use in horses, but not yet available for people.
- West Nile can't be transmitted from one person to another.

CHOLERA

Cholera is a highly communicable, waterborne and gastrointestinal disease. If the symptoms are reported in the early stages, the disease can be easily diagnosed and is curable. Cholera is caused by the bacterium *Vibrio choler*, which multiplies quickly in the intestine and produces a venomous liquid called cholera toxin (CTX). This liquid attaches to the walls of the intestine and interrupts the flow of body fluids in and out of the body. As a result, the body drains out an immense quantity of fluids in the form of diarrhea.

Means of Transmission

It takes about one million cholera bacteria to cause the disease. That sounds like a lot, but that much bacteria can be found in a glass of water that does not even look polluted. Unhygienic practices as well as unsanitary conditions promote the spread of the disease. Exposure to houseflies and domestic animals can also increase the chances of catching cholera because both can carry of the disease. However, the disease is not communicable, that is it cannot spread from person to the other.

 WORDS TO UNDERSTAND

eradicate: to get rid of something completely.
gastrointestinal: related to the stomach and intestines.
rehydration: to cause something to absorb water after being dehydrated.

Symptoms

The signs and symptoms of cholera usually appear after one or two days of infection, but sometimes they take only a few hours to develop. Diarrhea and vomiting are the first symptoms. Excessive and watery diarrhea can lead to dehydration, dry skin, and leaves the patient feeling extremely thirsty. Nausea, rapid pulse, muscle spasm, and cramps are a few other symptoms that a patient develops. The body temperature and blood pressure also drops.

Prevention and Cure

Cholera is a curable disease and can be prevented by medication and drinking plenty of fluids. It is advisable for patients to take oral **rehydration** solution (ORS) to replace bodily fluids. One should boil water before drinking, or drink bottled water. Practicing personal as well as environmental hygiene and sanitation can also help in preventing the spread of cholera. As the cholera bacteria are found in feces of patients, effective treatment of waste is necessary.

History of Cholera

Seven cholera pandemics have occurred in the past 200 years—all of them in Asia. Cholera is still endemic in more than 50 countries of the world. The first cholera pandemic outbreak in Asia occurred near the upper

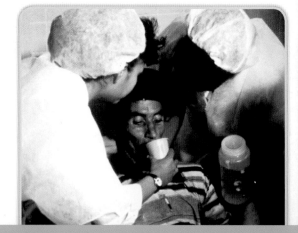

Ganges River, India, and lasted from 1817 to 1823. About 10,000 British troops, and hundreds of thousands of Indians died during this pandemic. Gradually, it spread to Thailand, Indonesia, Russia, and other Asian countries, killing tens of millions people worldwide.

Recent Cholera Outbreaks

In 1961, cholera sprouted in Indonesia and killed scores of people. The disease first discovered on the island of Sulawesi, then spread across the rest of Asia, to the Middle East, and reached Africa in 1971. The pandemic reached Italy in 1973 and claimed many lives. Another cholera outbreak occurred in 1991 in South America, more than a hundred years after it had been eradicated, and spread across the continent. Most recently, there were 815,000 cases of cholera in Haiti between 2010 and 2017. As of 2018, one of the worst cholera epidemics in history is raging in Yemen; experts predict that one million people will be affected, more than half of them children.

SIDEBAR: DID YOU KNOW?

- Robert Koch discovered the *Vibrio cholera bacterium* in 1883.

- *Cholera bacterium* is also found in coastal waters; it attaches to tiny sea animals called copepod.

YELLOW FEVER

Yellow fever is a viral infection spread by the bite of the infected Aedes mosquitoes. The virus enters the bloodstream of a mosquito and starts multiplying. When this infected mosquito bites a person the virus present in its salivary glands enters the human bloodstream, travels towards the lymph nodes, and multiplies there. Then the virus travels to the other parts of the body, such as the liver, and replicates.

Types of Transmission

Yellow fever is not infectious and cannot spread from one person to the other by direct contact. It is transmitted in three slightly different ways, depending on the location.

Jungle (Sylvatic) yellow fever usually occurs in tropical rainforests when the infected wild mosquitoes bite monkeys and spread the disease. Other mosquitoes then bite the infected monkeys and carry the infection. These infected mosquitoes bite people traveling in jungles, causing minor cases of yellow fever.

Intermediate yellow fever: Mosquitoes that breed in forests and near households cause intermediate yellow fever. They infect both monkeys and people. Contact between the infected mosquitoes and people induces the transmission of the disease.

WORDS TO UNDERSTAND

diagnose: to determine a medical illness by examination.
dengue fever: a viral disease that causes fever, chills, headache, and pain in the joints.
leptospirosis: a bacterial disease that is sometimes confused with yellow fever, due to similar symptoms.

Urban yellow fever: Urban populations can be infected on a big scale if an infected mosquito spreads the virus to unvaccinated people living in close quarters.

Three Stages

Early stage: lasts for three to four days.

Reduction stage: lasts a day; many people recover from this stage.

Last stage: comes after the reduction stage and can cause organ dysfunction, delirium, coma, shock, even death.

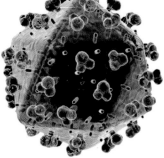

Yellow fever virus

Symptoms, Prevention, and Cure

It takes about three to six days for the yellow fever virus to develop inside the body and for the symptoms to appear. High fever, headache, muscle and joint ache are some of the early signs. Jaundice is also very common in patients down with yellow fever. They may suffer from loss of appetite, vomiting, and in extreme cases multi-organ failure, coma, and seizures. The disease is difficult to **diagnose** in its earlier stages and can be confused with malaria, **dengue**, **leptospirosis**, or viral hepatitis.

It is incurable and vaccination is the best way to prevent it. People should protect themselves from mosquito bites by using insect repellants and wearing full-length clothes.

1793 Epidemic

The yellow fever epidemic of 1793 was among worst epidemics ever in the United States. It became a scourge in Philadelphia, which was a key port city at the time, and about one-tenth of the population of the region perished. The disease kept occurring repeatedly and finally turned into an epidemic. It occurred in 1794, 1796, 1797, and 1798. Thousands of people died in the epidemic and by the end of 1798, more than half of the population left the city permanently, leaving merely 8,000 people.

1878 Epidemic

Yellow fever usually flourishes during spring, in rainy and humid weather. In the spring of 1878, the disease took a toll on the Caribbean people, especially the Cubans. After the civil war, thousands of refugees fled the island and came to New Orleans. The disease hit New Orleans in a big way, driving one-fifth of the population out of the city. In the Mississippi Valley, Memphis also witnessed thousands of deaths.

See a video about what happened when yellow fever struck Philadelphia in 1793.

SIDEBAR: DID YOU KNOW?

- There is a safe and effective vaccine for yellow fever.
- Yellow fever is still endemic in South America and sub-Saharan Africa.

TYPHUS

Yellow fever is a viral infection spread by the bite of the infected Aedes mosquitoes. Typhus is an infectious bacterial disease caused by one of the two Rickettsia bacteria—Rickettsia prowazekii or Rickettsia typhi. The bacteria were named after Dr. Howard Taylor Ricketts and Stanislaus Josef Mathias von Prowazek, who died from typhus while investigating its cause. Typhus is transmitted to people by the bite of an **arthropod**, such as lice and fleas. The bacteria enter the bloodstream and damage blood vessels, brain cells, the gastrointestinal tract, lungs, heart, and liver. It can remain infective in the feces of rodents for months and can easily spread into the atmosphere.

Types of Typhus

The type of typhus depends on which type of arthropod did the biting.
- Endemic (murine) typhus
- Epidemic (louse-borne) typhus
- Scrub (mite-borne) typhus
- Brill-Zinsser disease

Means of Transmission

Typhus does not spread directly from person to person. However, it can be transmitted by coming into contact with a person having body louse. Human body lice and rat fleabites are two of the main causes of the

WORDS TO UNDERSTAND

arthropod: an invertebrate with jointed legs, segmented body, and exoskeleton; includes insects and crustaceans.

louse: a small insect that lives on skin or fur (plural, lice).

murine: related to mice or other rodents.

transmission of typhus. Poor personal hygiene, unhygienic surroundings, and poor sanitation increase the chances of typhus transmission.

Symptoms, Prevention, and Cure

It takes about one to two weeks for the signs and symptoms to appear in the body. Very high fever along with severe headache and skin rashes are two of the earliest symptoms. Abdominal and muscle pain, nausea, dry cough, vomiting, and loss of appetite are some of the common signs. To prevent typhus from spreading, people should take care of

personal hygiene as well as the hygiene and sanitation of their surroundings. They should use insect repellents, insecticides, and rodent-control measures. Wearing full-length clothing and sleeping under mosquito nets to protect one from mosquitoes and other insect bites is advisable. Getting vaccination is also one of the ways to prevent typhus.

History of Typhus

Typhus epidemics were man-made, in the sense that poor sanitary conditions led to the spread of the disease. By the 18th century, typhus became an epidemic in Europe, Russia, Africa, and the Middle East. The epidemic wiped out Napoleon Bonaparte's army in 1812. Napoleon invaded Russia with 600,000 soldiers and only around 30,000 survived; far more were killed by typhus than by enemy soldiers. Endemic typhus was also called "jail fever" since it became common among prisoners due to unhygienic conditions of the crowded prison cells. In Ireland between 1816 and 1819, the disease hit hard during a famine. It reoccurred in 1846 after the failure of the potato crop and killed a large number of people.

Typhus in Serbia and Russia

When World War I broke out in 1914, a typhus epidemic also broke out in Serbia. Around 150,000 Serbian soldiers died of typhus in 1915. About 30,000 Austrian prisoners of war and medical staff died from typhus in Serbian prisons. The typhus epidemic reached Russia during that country's civil war. From 1917 to 1925, it caused the death of about three million people and left about 25 million people infected. During World War II, German concentration camps were also badly hit by the epidemic.

SIDEBAR: DID YOU KNOW?

- Another type of rickettsial infection carried by human lice is called trench fever. The name comes from the fact that it was discovered among soldiers fighting in trenches.

- Charles Nicolle was a French bacteriologist who won the Nobel Prize for discovering that lice are the main carrier of typhus.

SMALLPOX

Smallpox is a contagious and often deadly disease that causes rashes on the skin. A virus known as Variola causes smallpox. There are two types of variola viruses—variola major and variola minor. Humans are the only natural hosts of the virus. The variola virus enters the body and settles in the throat, where it mixes with saliva. It invades the cells that make up the body and multiplies in large numbers. It then breaks out of the cells and can make the infected person very ill.

Means of Transmission

Smallpox is a very infectious disease and transmits rapidly among people. The virus spreads when an infected person sneezes, coughs, or comes in close contact with others. Inhaling the air around the patient and sharing his food, utensils, towels, bed linen, and other items, also transmit smallpox.

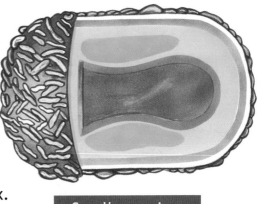

Small pox virus

Symptoms

It takes about two weeks for signs and symptoms to develop after infection. High fever up to 104°F (40°C), headache, backache, and achy muscles are some of the early symptoms of smallpox. The infected

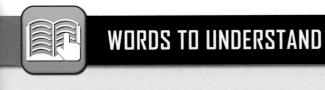

WORDS TO UNDERSTAND

antibody: a substance produced by the body to fight infections and diseases; also the most important part of the immune system.

immunization: the practice of giving people vaccines to make them better able to resist particular illnesses.

malaise: the feeling of being generally unwell.

person also develops small pus-filled blisters, which turn into sores and become crusty after eight to nine days. **Malaise**, weakness, and fatigue are also very common in smallpox patients.

Prevention and Treatment

Vaccination is one of the easiest ways to prevent smallpox. However, people who have been infected by the smallpox virus 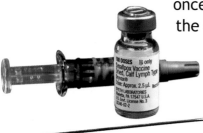 once never suffer from the disease again. This is because their bodies make **antibodies** when exposed to the virus, and the antibodies fight off the disease if the virus strikes again.

The First Smallpox Pandemic

The Antonine Plague was one of the biggest ancient pandemics; it raged from 165 to 180 AD. It was also called the "Plague of Galen" because Galen, a great Roman physician, was the one who described it. The Antonine Plague my have been a smallpox pandemic, although there is a chance that it was measles. In any case, it reached the Roman Empire through military troops and then spread to other places. The pandemic reached Asia Minor, Greece, Egypt, and Italy, killing millions of people around the world.

In the 10th century, a practice called variolation was developed in China and India. In variolation, small amount of pus is taken from smallpox blisters and injected into a healthy person. This causes mild illness but it makes the person permanently immune to the disease. However, variolation was a risky procedure and could even cause death.

Smallpox Pandemic in Europe

Smallpox reached Europe between the fifth and seventh centuries and became a frequent epidemic during the middle ages. It spread rapidly among the European populations before reaching America, Mexico, Canada, and other areas. The disease killed 30 percent of the people it infected. About 300 million people succumbed to the disease in the 20th century. But thanks to a successful global immunization campaign, smallpox was eradicated. The last known case of smallpox was reported in Somalia in 1977.

The Invention of Vaccines

In the late 18th century, there were reports that milkmaids who had contracted a similar disease, called cowpox, were immune to smallpox. To test this theory, a doctor named Edward Jenner took a small amount of pus from a milkmaid suffering from cowpox and injected it into James Phipps, a young boy. In 1796, Jenner concluded that acquiring cowpox provided immunity

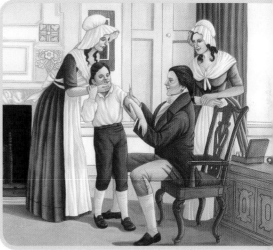

against smallpox. He published his results in 1798 and coined the word "vaccine" from the Latin word vacca, which means "cow."

SIDEBAR: DID YOU KNOW?

- In the 18th century, smallpox was known as the "speckled monster."

- Although people do not get smallpox any more, the World Health Organization and the U.S. government still keep supplies of smallpox vaccines, in case the disease is ever revived.

POLIO

Poliomyelitis, or polio, is a contagious viral disease that can lead to partial or full **paralysis**, brain damage, and in severe cases, death. Poliovirus attacks the central nervous system. The virus enters through the mouth and nose and multiplies in the throat and the intestinal tract. It is then absorbed by, and spread through, blood and the lymph system. It multiplies in the lymph nodes in the intestinal tract and releases into the bloodstream.

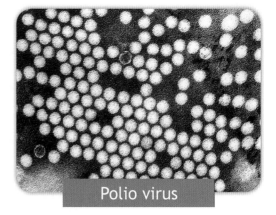
Polio virus

Means of Transmission

Polio can transmit from one person to the other via respiratory droplets, and nasal and oral secretions. Polio virus is also present in the feces of infected people, and inadequate waste management increases the chances of infections. Drinking contaminated water, and practicing poor personal and environmental hygiene help the transmission of the disease.

Types of Infections

In the vast majority of polio cases, no signs and symptoms appear, although the person can still infect someone else. This is called

 WORDS TO UNDERSTAND

corrective: therapeutic.
incurable: describes a disease for which there's no cure.
paralysis: the inability to move.
subclinical: refers to an infection or illness that is so mild that it has no symptoms.

subclinical polio. The other types of polio are non-paralytic and paralytic infections. In non-paralytic cases, patients suffer from sore throat, headache, respiratory tract infections, fatigue, body stiffness, and body ache. Only about one percent of cases are of the paralytic type, which is the most serious. Fever, headache, difficulty in breathing, sore throat, and stiffness in the neck and back along with severe muscle pain are common signs and symptoms of paralytic polio.

Treatment and Prevention

Polio is an incurable disease. However, it can be prevented by vaccination. Inactivated Polio Vaccine (IPV) and Oral Polio Vaccine (OPV) are two of the most recommended polio vaccines. Patients should wear braces or corrective shoes to help in walking. Exercise or physical activities increase the muscle strength and functions of the body.

Polio in the Past

The disease has existed since ancient times. However, it broke out only in small

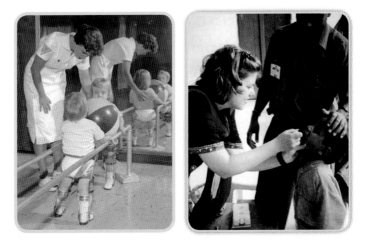

numbers until the 20th century. In the United States, small polio outbreaks began to occur in the 1900s. Soon the disease turned into epidemics in Europe, Asia, North America, and Australia. In 1916, polio was considered an epidemic since thousands of people suffered from it in the US. The major epidemics occurred in the 1940s and the 1950s.

However, the epidemic of 1952 was considered the worst of all since it infected about 58,000 people and killed more than 3,000.

Polio Vaccine

The principle of vaccination states that if the body is exposed to a harmless form of a disease-causing microorganism, it will produce antibodies to fight off that microorganism. Dr. Jonas Salk, an immunologist, observed that immunity could be achieved by injecting harmless, noninfectious, and inanimate viruses in the body. He developed a vaccine with inanimate poliovirus and first tested it on monkeys, and then on children already suffering from polio. Salk also tested the vaccine on himself, his wife and children, and several volunteers. None of them developed any side effects. In 1955, the polio vaccine was made available to public.

Polio Today

Thanks to the vaccine, most countries have stopped the spread of the disease completely. Only Afghanistan, Nigeria, and Pakistan have been unable to end polio in their countries. Still, there were only 37 cases reported in 2016.

SIDEBAR: DID YOU KNOW?

- People whose chest muscles became paralyzed due to polio were put in an iron lung, which was a type of ventilator that helped them breathe.

- Some doctors in the 1950s felt that the polio hysteria was overblown. They pointed out that while more than 3,000 people died of polio in 1952, about 34,000 died of tuberculosis in the same year.

SARS

Severe Acute Respiratory Syndrome (SARS) is a **respiratory** viral illness caused by the SARS coronavirus (SARS-CoV). The coronavirus gets its name from its appearance. When viewed under a microscope, it appears to have a halo or crown. SARS is a serious form of pneumonia and is highly **communicable**. Research shows that SARS-CoV can live months or years outside the body when the temperature is below freezing point.

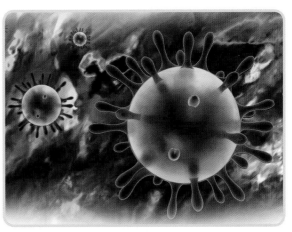

How Does it Spread?

The virus attacks the respiratory tract and multiplies in the cells of the host bodies. It invades the host cells and ultimately kills them. The viral attack causes the immune system to rapidly release more white blood cells than the body can produce. After infecting the respiratory tract, the invaders reach the lungs and cause severe respiratory illness.

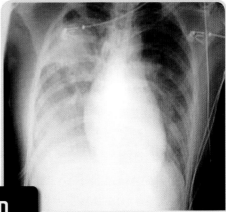

 WORDS TO UNDERSTAND

communicable: easily spread from person to person.

hygiene: the practice of keeping oneself and one's surroundings clean in order to avoid infections and diseases.

respiratory: having to do with breathing.

Means of Transmission

The SARS virus may live on hands, tissues, and other surfaces for up to six hours as droplets and up to three hours after the droplets have dried. It can be transmitted by coming into close contact with persons suffering from SARS. When an infected person coughs or sneezes, the infected droplets spread into the air and the virus spreads by the inhalation of, or by touching, those particles. Coming into direct contact with the body fluids or nasal secretions of the patient, and hugging, touching, or kissing spread the disease. Even sharing food, drinks, and utensils, or using the same washrooms and towels increase the chances of transmission.

Prevention and Cure

People should avoid coming in direct contact with those suffering from SARS, or traveling to places where the disease is rampant. Practicing personal hygiene such as washing hands frequently, especially before and after meals, and after using the bathroom prevents transmission. The mouth should always be covered while coughing or sneezing. Avoid sharing food, drinks, or utensils with infected persons and clean commonly touched surfaces such as doorknobs, light switches, etc., with a disinfectant. If possible, people should wear masks, goggles, and gloves to avoid catching the infection.

Symptoms of SARS

The symptoms of SARS start appearing about two to ten days after coming into contact with the virus. A person can be infected again even if he has recovered from the illness. Sore throat, dry cough, headache, high fever, chills, difficulty in breathing, ache in the body and muscles, and pneumonia are some common symptoms of SARS.

SARS Outbreaks

SARS was first reported in Foshan City, in the Guangdong Province of China in November 2002. The Chinese government took some actions to control the sudden outbreak of SARS, but neither the government acknowledged the outbreak nor did it inform the World Health Organization. The Chinese health ministry reported 305 cases of SARS and five deaths in February 2003.

How Did it Spread?

Initially, Chinese healthcare officials thought that SARS spreads through droplet transmission. People infected with the disease release infected droplets into the air when they cough or sneeze. When other people inhale these droplets, it can make them contract the virus. However, SARS spreads very quickly, which means that the disease can also spread through small aerosol particles that can be breathed in by people. Such particles can travel over great distances and can stay in the air far longer than the infected droplets.

SARS in China

Over a period of few months, SARS spread to the other parts of China. The venue for the women's World Cup tournament (2003), which was supposed to take place in China, was shifted to the United States of America because of the SARS epidemic. The International Ice Hockey Federation (IIHF) also cancelled the IIHF Women's World Championship (2003) that was to take place in Beijing. By now, SARS had turned into an epidemic—it was spreading quickly. Schools and other public organizations closed throughout Hong Kong and Singapore.

Outside China

SARS spread outside China quickly. A WHO physician, Dr. Carlo Urbani, reported several cases of an unusual type of pneumonia at the hospital where he worked. One of his patients was a businessman who had traveled from the Guangdong province of China through Hong Kong, to Hanoi in Vietnam. Both the businessman and the doctor stayed in the same Metropole Hotel and spread the infection among the hotel staff and guests. The businessman, however, could not survive and succumbed to the illness. The healthcare workers who treated the businessman also fell ill. Dr. Urbani identified SARS but eventually died of the disease in March 2003.

Around the World

SARS spread to over a dozen countries within a short span and infected thousands of people around the world, including those living in Asia, Australia, Europe, Africa, North and South Americas. It reached about 29 countries and claimed more than lives. The disease infected more than 8,000 people worldwide. No cases have been reported since, but SARS is still considered to be a dangerous agent that could pose a threat to public health in the future.

SIDEBAR: DID YOU KNOW?

- **SARS is caused by a member of the coronavirus family that is also responsible for causing the common cold.**
- **The virus causing SARS was named by the WHO in April 2003.**

GLOBAL HEALTH ORGANIZATIONS

Viruses and bacteria do not recognize borders, which makes public health a shared global responsibility. Many international health organizations conduct surveys and publish reports informing health care professionals and the general public about global diseases and health statistics. They help to promote global health by providing expert advice and health aid. The most significant of these groups is probably the World Health Organization (WHO).

World Health Organization

The WHO is a health agency of the United Nations, and it's responsible for matters relating to public health around the world. It aims at building a healthier world and assists governments worldwide in strengthening health services and providing necessary aids during emergencies. Since its inception in 1948, the WHO has been waging a war against epidemics and pandemics worldwide, especially in the developing countries. It also develops international standards for food and pharmaceutical products. The WHO works in partnership with other organizations and spreads awareness concerning nutrition, health precautions, drug addiction, and sexual and reproductive health.

WORDS TO UNDERSTAND

forecasting: predicting or estimating.

precautionary: preventive.

resistance: here, refers to the ability of the body to fight off infection.

Fighting Pandemics: Steps by Health Organizations and World Governments

Forecasting a Pandemic

Forecasting the potential threat of an infectious disease plays a crucial role in controlling pandemics. It gives health organizations and authorities the required time to decide upon the preventive measures and frame their plan of action. They frame their public health orders by understanding scientifically how the infection spreads. A detailed study of pandemics that occurred in the past gives them information about the possible aftermaths of a disease and the necessary steps required to combat it.

Precautionary Measures

Precautionary measures are the fundamental measures taken by health authorities aimed at reducing the transmission of the pathogen by preventing contact. In severe emergencies, they isolate the infected individuals and keep them in quarantine under strict medical supervision, so that there is a reduced risk of infecting the rest of the population. For example, the Singapore government controlled the spread of SARS in 2003, which killed about 800 people worldwide, by taking precautionary measures against the infected people. Various national and international health organizations collaborate with each other in notifying and controlling the diseases.

Increasing Natural Resistance

In the period before and during the spread of a pandemic, health organizations use various channels to educate the public about the importance of, and ways to increase, their natural **resistance**. People are encouraged to maintain personal and general hygiene, have a balanced and nutritious diet, and avoid nervous and physical exhaustion to reduce their susceptibility to the disease.

International Health Regulations

The increased overseas travel in present times also increases the mobility of a contagious disease and increases risks for a global pandemic. The WHO, in collaboration with the governments worldwide, has formulated and implemented many international health regulations. In some cases, the international air travel of those infected with a disease is restricted to avoid its spread. Several countries have made it compulsory for people to be vaccinated against certain diseases.

SIDEBAR: DID YOU KNOW?

- According to the WHO's *World Health Report,* public spending on health services benefits the rich more than the poor who actually need those services.

- If the existing preventive measures are used efficiently, it can reduce the global burden of diseases by as much as 70 percent.

WORLD PANDEMICS DATA

HIV/AIDS
Number of People Living with HIV/AIDS, 2016

East and Southern Africa: 19.4 million

Western and Central Africa: 6.1 million

Asia and Pacific: 5.1 million

Western and Central Europe and North America: 2.1 million

Latin American and Caribbean: 2.1 million

Eastern Europe and Central Asia: 1.6 million

Middle East and North Africa: 230,000

Northern America

Caribbean

Central America

South America

Source:
UNAIDS Data 2017

Northern Europe

Eastern Europe

Western
Europe

Central
Europe

Central Asia

Southern
Europe

Middle East

Eastern Asia

Northern Africa

Western
Africa

Western Asia

South-Eastern Asia

Southern Asia

Central Africa

Eastern Africa

Melanesia

Southern Africa

Australia and New Zealand

WORLD PANDEMICS DATA

AVIAN INFLUENZA

Total Number of Human Cases Reported to WHO, 2003-2017

COUNTRY	CASES	DEATHS
Azerbaijan	8	5
Bangladesh	8	1
Cambodia	56	37
Canada	1	1
China	53	31
Djibouti	1	0
Egypt	359	120
Indonesia	200	168
Iraq	3	2
Lao People's Democratic Republic	2	2
Myanmar	1	0
Nigeria	1	1
Pakistan	3	1
Thailand	25	17
Turkey	12	4
Vietnam	127	64

Source:
World Health Organization,
Global Health Observatory, 2018

WORLD PANDEMICS DATA

MALARIA

Population of Areas at High Risk for Malaria, By Region 2017

Africa:	749,142,318
Americas:	22,401,461
Eastern Mediterranean:	117,606,110
Southeast Asia:	190,882,348
Western Pacific:	33,000,383
TOTAL:	1,113,032,620

CHOLERA

Cases of Cholera Reported to WHO, 2016

COUNTRY	CASES	COUNTRY	CASES
Afghanistan	677	Malawi	1,792
Angola	78	Mozambique	883
Australia	1	Myanmar	782
Benin	761	Nepal	169
Burundi	434	Netherlands	1
Canada	1	Niger	38
China	27	Nigeria	768
Congo	15	Philippines	124
Democratic Republic of the Congo	28,093	Republic of Korea	4
		Rwanda	355
Denmark	1	Somalia	15,619
Dominican Republic	1,159	South Sudan	4,295
Germany	1	Thailand	52
Ghana	175	Uganda	516
Haiti	41,421	United Kingdom of Great Britain and Northern Ireland	19
India	841	
Iraq	35	United Republic of Tanzania	11,360
Japan	10	United States of America	14
Kenya	5,866	Yemen	15,751
		Zimbabwe	10

Source:
World Health Organization,
Global Health Observatory, 2018

TEXT-DEPENDENT QUESTIONS

1. What is the difference between an epidemic and a pandemic?

2. What is the name of the virus that causes AIDS?

3. Can you contract AIDS from hugging someone with the disease?

4. How is nutrition related to HIV/AIDS?

5. How is the flu spread?

6. What were some of the impacts of the 1918 flu epidemic?

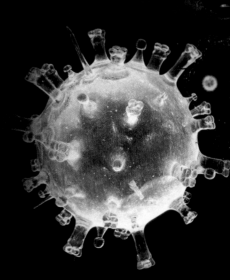

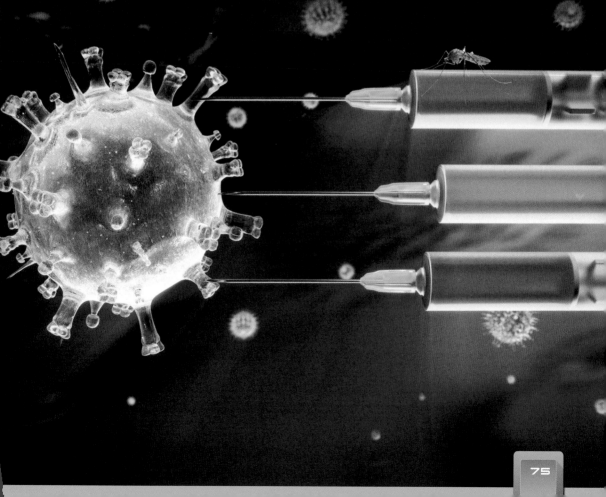

7. How is malaria spread?

8. What causes cholera?

9. What are the symptoms of plague?

10. Who was Edward Jenner?

RESEARCH PROJECTS

1. Using the information in this book and additional research create a timeline of the HIV/AIDS epidemic, beginning with the first cases in the 1980s and continuing through today. Include data about infection rates as well as about access to treatment.

2. Find out more about how to prevent illnesses such as those listed in this book. What steps can people take to keep themselves healthier? Make a poster to educate others about what you have learned.

3. Find out more about one of the researchers mentioned in this book whose work interests you. It could be ancient Roman physician Galen, Alphonse Laveran, Edward Jenner, Jonas Salk, or some other researcher. What were their lives like? How did they go about their research and how did the general public react to it?

4. Find out more about daily life during one of the pandemics discussed, such as the Black Death, the Spanish flu, or one of the yellow fever epidemics. Write a short story from the perspective of someone living through one of these situations.

FURTHER READING

Anderson, T. Neill. *People of the Plague: The Philadelphia Flu Epidemic*. Boston, MA: Charlesbridge, 2014.

Diamond, Jared. *Guns, Germs, and Steel*. Twentieth Anniversary Edition. New York: W.W. Norton, 2017.

Furgang, Adam. *Smallpox*. New York: Rosen, 2010.

Jarrow, Gail. *Bubonic Panic: When Plague Invaded America*. Honesdale, PA: Calkins Creek, 2016.

INTERNET RESOURCES

Contagion: Historical Views of Diseases and Epidemics.
http://ocp.hul.harvard.edu/contagion/
Harvard University's Open Collections Program hosts this site, which has articles, timelines, and documents related to epidemics in history.

HIV/AIDS and Teens FAQ
https://teens.webmd.com/hiv-aids-and-teens-faq#1
This site from Web MD asks and answers many important questions about HIV/AIDS.

Outbreaks: Protecting Americans from Infectious Diseases.
http://healthyamericans.org/reports/outbreaks2015/
A report from Trust for America's Health on epidemic preparations at the state level.

Picture Credits:

INDEX

INDEX